A Certain Way

Mona Dash

For my parents-in-law:

Dr K.C.Misra, in your memory
Mrs Bimolprabha Ratho, for your love of poetry

A Certain Way

Mona Dash

Skylark Publications UK

First Edition: A Certain Way
First published in Great Britain in 2017 by:
Skylark Publications UK
10 Hillcross Avenue
Morden
Surrey SM4 4EA
www.Skylarkpublications.co.uk

This book is sold subject to the condition that it shall not, by way of trade or otherwise, be lent, re-sold, hired out, or otherwise circulated without the author's and publisher's prior consent in any form of binding or cover other than that in which it is published and without a similar condition including this condition being imposed on the subsequent purchaser.

Mona Dash has asserted her right under the Copyright, Designs and Patents Act 1988 to be identified as the author of this work.

©2017 Mona Dash

ISBN 978-0-9560840-4-0

British Library Cataloguing in Publication Data. A CIP record for this book can be obtained from the British Library.

Designed and typeset by Skylark Publications UK.
Cover design by Yogesh Patel

Cover photograph: Goutam Das

Acknowledgements

Gratitude for helping this collection come to life:

Yogesh Patel, ever versatile, publisher, poet, friend, mentor, guide for announcing the crowd funding initiative by Word Masala and awarding the 'poet of achievement award' to me in a ceremony in the House of Lord's in 2016. Thank you for patiently answering my questions, thank you for publishing this collection!

My very first pre-subscribers of this collection, the no-questions-asked buyers, my friends – Jagdish Mahapatra, Ajit Panda, Suman Giri, A. Surendra Kumar, Koushik Chatterjee, Prashant Panda, Binod Panda. Also, to eminent poet: Reginald Massey for being one of the first poet-critic to subscribe and Dr Jagdish Dave (MBE).

Usha Kishore, poet, friend, mentor for your support and help in structuring and editing and for all the encouragement, many thanks.

I would also like to thank the poets whose support I was fortunate to have:

Mamata Dash for reading each of the poems just after it was written

Debjani Chatterjee MBE for the first editorial input on my Ms

Saleem Peeradina for reading the editorial input and writing the blurb comments

Jaydeep Sarangi for the encouragement and publishing

Shree Rajendra Kishore Panda for the quiet encouragement

Also to Shanta Acharya, Atreya Surma Uppalari , Sunil Sharma and Kavita Jindal for support

And my dear family and friends, UCE '93 group, London Met MA Creative Writing 2014, for your support in my journey with words, for all the likes and encouragement.

I acknowledge and thank the following editors for publishing my work.

Journals : *Kavya Bharati, India, The Lake, UK, Muse India, Episteme, India, LakeView International, Moondance, USA, The Black Rose,UK, The Journal UK, Exiled Writer's Ink, UK, Poetry 24, The Dhauli Review, India.*

Anthologies: *Home Thoughts (Cyberwit, 2017), Searching for the Sublime:Poems from Australia and India (Cyberwit, 2016 (The Dance of the peacock (Hidden Brook Press, Canada, 2013), Suvarnarekha (The Poetry society of India, 2014), Foreign encounters, Just Met anthology (2014) Just Met Anthology (2013), In this Life (United Press 2004), Bright Voices (United Press 2003), and 'Love across a broken map' (Dahlia Publications UK, 2016).*

Contents

A Certain Way	10
Belonging	12
The Skin of Tradition	13
Suitcases	15
Διασπορά	17
Rejection	19
The Immigrant's Song	21
Nostalgic Rain	22
Home and Beyond	23
Language	24
Creator	25
Durga	26
Shiva	28
The God of Happiness	29
Shrine	30
Wholeness	31
Prayer	32
Destiny	33
Despair	34
Whispers	35
Atonement	36
Nowhere to Go	37
Woman	38
The Punishment	39
Metamorphosis	42
Nympheas	43
Opera Garnier	44
Aquarelle Flash	46
The Passage of Time	47
Konarak Express	49
Thirty Kilometres	50
Stranger Love	51
A Call	53

The Glass Jar	54
Of the Night	56
A Fair Exchange	58
Blighted Knight	59
Happiness in Love	60
His Poem	61
His Gift	63
Love Lost	65
Ill-Fated Love	67
Nostalgia	68
Jealousy	69
Midlife Crisis	71
Perfection	72
Childlessness	73
My Children	74
Advice to My Unborn Daughter	75
Motherhood	77
Carousel	78
In Search of Balance	79
Kiss of Tragedy	80
Words	81
We Write in Vain	83
Dreams	85
Ruins	86
What is Lost	87
In Memory	88
Shiver up a Spine	90
People, Unlike Fish	92
The Visit	93
Immersion	95

Mona Dash is an Indian writer settled in London. With an education in Telecoms Engineering and Management from Odisha, she works as a sales manager in a leading global technology organisation. She writes fiction and poetry and her work has been anthologised widely and published in international journals. She has a Masters in Creative Writing (with distinction) from the London Metropolitan University.

She is also working towards a PhD in Area Studies.

She has read poetry and fiction at literary festivals and poetry venues such as The Nehru Centre, Lauderdale House and Leicester Writes. She has also read her poems at the House of Lords.

Also by Mona Dash

'Dawn-drops' is her first collection of poetry published by Writer's Workshop, India.

Her first book of fiction 'Untamed Heart' was published by Tara India Research Press in 2016.

A Certain Way

As an immigrant,
I am expected to behave in a way,
a certain way.

Colour the walls with turmeric,
fill my soul with lament
for the land whose shores I have left
to become richer economically
poorer emotionally.
Fold oil into long black hair,
dream the stars of the eastern skies,
in this land, the land I call my own,
but never to be my own.
Wrapped in sarees, sapphire blue, *sindoor* red,
meant to be nostalgic about the
monsoon spray dazzling my eyes
calming my burning skin.

Instead, my mind
soothed by the nourishing cool green
of the land I live in,
energised by the glowing orange sun
of the land I come from,
decorates ice cubes with spice.

With silver anklets, red stilettoes,
the shortest, blackest dress,
I sip prosecco, spear olives expertly,
pile plates with rice and chicken curry
while in the garden
lavender, jasmine, clematis, and marigold,
spread their roots, dance their petals
into the pale grey wet skies
and the searing sunshine.

Uproot, grow, take root
parallel truths, a little of this,
a little of that.
For an immigrant,
there is no certain way to be.

Sindoor red - vermillion red

Belonging

Corporate men, pinstripe suits
in deep discussion, in accents
lilting French, baritone German, twangy American.
Among them an Indian, worse, a woman, Indian.

When I speak in tone, walk with the step
eyebrows raise, they lean forward to hear better,
talk louder when addressing me, as if I am deaf
telling me silently:
You shouldn't be here.

A crowded English pub, people
standing in spaces too small for them.
I order the drinks.
The bartender stares when I say
'A glass of red wine and three pints of lager'
looking confused, leaning forward closer
telling me silently:
You shouldn't be here.

Welcoming smiles, women in sarees,
grinding *masalas*, rolling *chapatis*,
television is the world, content
in the four walls, within set boundaries.
My hometown, my roots, so far from my branches.
Ill at ease I sit
listening to my own voice
telling me silently:
You shouldn't be here.

Masalas: spices
Chapatis: Indian bread

The Skin of Tradition

1

The foreigner watches a wedding in fascination
large *bindi* squatting on her forehead
red saree colouring white limbs.
The elders enthuse how she
sits relaxed on the dusty ground
reveres the sacredness of every chant
embraces chaos in wondrous happiness.

The Americans, Germans, English,
French, Italians flock here, hearts one
with conch shells; cross-legged,
slurp white rice and dal from banana leaves.
Yet I, I ask for my fork and spoon.
Yet I, born in a small town, tempered by heat,
coloured with tradition, married saree-clad
in front of the fire, complain of the fumes
my eyes burning. I, brought up within these walls
makes it a point to question too much
why should I, why must I, bow in respect,
hide in shame, follow rules and customs,
forget myself. I question for years.

Later, in London, that city I call home,
forgetting, at home *tulsi* plants sit in courtyards
white *chita* is drawn on Thursday
to welcome Lakshmi.
'A city without temples scratching its skyline
cannot be home ever,' they pronounce.
I question for years.

2

The answer, thought but not mouthed:
You can appreciate culture,
fold your legs in suppliance
bend your head, fast all day in a temple
knowing tomorrow you will be home.
Today is a thrill, like climbing Machu Picchu
like rowing down the Okavango delta.
When the blood that runs in you today
bled on a pyre, hundreds of years ago
soaking chrysanthemum garlands
when a village is somewhere, had you lived
fifty years before, you would be
behind a veil waiting, watching,
when not that many years back, a marriage
marked you with blood red *sindoor* in black hair
closeted rooms, opened legs
breeding healthy sons and if not white widows.

When you know all this, then, the legs don't fold here
in the dust, in the sacredness
even though they do at Yoga in the gym.

The heart that belongs, never accepting, runs,
runs the farthest,
to shed centuries of old skin.

Suitcases

battered suitcases
tightly packed, transoceanic
oversized chocolate tins, shortbread
spirits, perfumes duty free
lego, whittard teas
fortnum mason jams, l'occitane lotions
nestling in muslin gift bags

gifts rationed
familial smiles, knowing shrugs
for everything is here
zara, mango, earl grey, body shop
chanel, yes everything
the world is here
the shelves are full

unspoken words
why did you leave
why did you love other lands
thoughts refracting
prisms, chants in minds
betrayal, traitor, traitor

smells, airs
living in another world
deciding between worlds
smoothly blend in? nourish identity?
gauged, studied, here, there
a single comment
opening Pandora boxes
of reactions

they go, they come
unknowing, large suitcases
migratory birds, looking for homes.

Διασπορά

The place we live in
has a name
no geography, no laws

                                          The contours touch
                                          several boundaries
                                          suspended over oceans

The inhabitants
straddle worlds, legs in one
minds in the other
souls here

                                          Emblems of countries
                                          in red, blue and black
                                          disparate identities

In this drifting space
sometimes we tilt
we shift towards
where we came from
sometimes we sink
into new lands

Floating, disjointed
mass
no names, no roots
only a scattering
seeds swept by a tuft of
hair
a dispersion

Diaspora

Rejection

The answer will be the same,
when the reply arrives
when the email opens
carefully worded words.
English polite.

'Thank you for submitting,
but it isn't for us.'

'No, it isn't for me
try somewhere else
knock elsewhere, beg further
for whatever you have
is not welcome.'

'We are busy with the volume of submissions.
Individual feedback cannot be given, regretfully.'

If something is not wanted, is it worth it?

The reply will be the same
consistently polite,
meaningfully rude.
Go away from our doors
with your benedictions
fragile words arranged in a pyramid
destined to never stand.
Feel free to carry your offerings
to other lands.

The land I come from
says sorry, we want to be more than what we are.
We can't have you, as you remind us of us
you stink of the familiar.

The land I live in
says sorry you are not smelling enough of
the land you come from, you remind us of us.
You need to be more different.

Neither here, nor there.

The email will be the same in its reply.
Chocolate covered prickles
consistently polite,
meaningfully rude.

The Immigrant's Song

When it rains here,
in this country, with its dark earth,
rainbow gardens,
sometimes the flecks of rain
touch the earth just like in the dusty Indian plains.
Fresh waters soak into the hungry soil.

The smell! Like when clouds break and it's monsoon
in India, the heat of the plains dissolving in the waters.
The smell of long ago, the smell of home.

Suddenly, this country with its different skies
roses in the summer, lights in the winter,
becomes home, as well.

Nostalgic Rain

An almost tropical rain arrives,
I watch from the window.
Quiet roads, quieter cars.
The almost tropical rain
adorns the hanging planters.
Colourful flowers, petunias, azaleas, fuchsias
but fragrance less,
so the rain awakens nothing, hidden.
There's even a hint of hailstones in today's rain.

But, to be truly tropical you
need to emerge from the hunger of heat
the acridity of drought.
You need to rise deep from ponds brimming with
lotuses
form clouds that spray down at will, lustily.
An almost tropical thunder today.

But to be truly tropical you
need to have been conceived in despair
spawned in hunger.
You need to have it in your belly.

The rain beats down today,
my silence
it is not the same.

Home and Beyond

There are many in this city
upon Westminster Bridge
who think if still
in the country they came from,
the one with the narrow roads,
smaller communities, they would be happier
bigger, treasured.

Life would have none of this
toiling, commuting, cooking meals for one,
waiting in queues, working at a desk, working on a desk.
It wouldn't happen in the country they came from
where the frangipani breathes, where the fish glisten,
where the mangoes are warm, where the rain is fragrant.

Forgetting they were the ones who decided to leave
the country of the narrow roads and claustrophobia
the lack of wealth, the lack of ideas, the lack of everything
forgetting they came to embrace a city, make love in her beauty
forgetting they could have looked and found more, back there.

The beauty there, the beauty here
both unnoticed by unseeing eyes
both ignored by accusing hearts.

Language

You are amused
when you hear words mispronounced
Preeface, instead of *preface*.

You are surprised
when you hear words unknown
and wonder how my alien tongue speaks
the language you made, nurtured.
What the rulers spoke
the brown sahibs learnt
the passport to jobs, money, life.

Don't you remember, when you came
and stayed three hundred years?
When you taught us to speak like you do?
When we spoke, the words were different
tempered by mustard, coloured with turmeric.
The language the same, the sound a foreigner.

You expect me to sound the same as you.
You are surprised I speak your language.

Many hundred years before
you had arrived in the land
cooked by the sun, garnished with spice,
decorated with jewels,
arrived and stayed, moving on bit by bit
conquering our minds, hearts, soil.

We made our changes, we learnt our lessons,
our tongues remained the same
foreign words our own.

Creator

Your first born
was grotesque
Arms spanning the world
crushing it with iron strength.
Your second born
was fierce
exploding fire from his mouth
burning souls in a day.

The ones who came after
and after
raged for days
destroying the fabric of the skies
the foundations of forests
ripping sturdy mountains
until the streams dripped blood.

Still, you didn't stop.

You carried on
producing offspring

one after the other
advancing across geographies
changing histories
living unimagined futures.

Until one day, they swallowed the sun
whole, shredded the earth
and washed away the paintings
of your image
Until one day they brought apocalypse
in the middle of the *Yuga*.[1]

Durga

It was only for an instant
that she forgot to breathe.
At that moment
the seas sucked through and dried
leaving craters of drought.
Hearts collapsed, exploded
pralaya in our lives.
Perversions took human form
as men, demon-like
gouged and penetrated.
Women ruptured into
mangled, grieving parts.
Stones, blades, rusty hammers
lodged in fragile bodies.

Durga! Mother!
Singhabahini!

She forgot to see
her eyes shut for a moment
and at that instant
the world was sucked into
the writhing abdomen of the
asuras.

Those lustrous eyes will open
benedictions shower
as we chant to Her.

Durga! Mother!
Singhabahini!

New worlds live.

Reference for 'Creator'

[1] **Yuga:** *an epoch or era within a four age cycle. A complete **Yuga** cycle starts with the age of Truth and righteousness (Satya **Yuga**), then the second age, when diseases are rampant and people are weaker (**Dwapara Yuga**), leading to the third age when virtue diminishes slightly (Treta **Yuga**), and -finally the age of darkness (**Kali Yuga**). The Yugas are meant to continue one after the other, and destruction, i.e apocalypse, comes at the end of it.*

Reference for 'Durga'

Pralaya: *cyclical destruction of the Universe which comes at the end of a Yuga.*

Yuga : *an epoch or era within a four age cycle.*

Singhabahini: *another name for Goddess Durga, the Supreme Mother and Goddess of creation. She slew the evil demon Mahisasura astride a lion, and hence the epithet Singha(lion) bahini(astride)*

Asura: *In Hindu mythology, demons are called Asuras. It is also a term used in most Indian languages to describe an especially evil human being, somewhat like the word monster. Physically asuras are very ugly, grotesque and have crude sensibilities. Asuras is the plural of asura.*

.

Shiva

Creator, destroyer, passive, fierce,
contradictions live in you, mirroring
the world around, praying to you.
A giver of boons, of wishes
indiscriminately perhaps.

Your devotees surround your form
snakes coil on your neck.
We bow to the
ash smeared, unwashed ascetic
Lord of Dance.

You live here as well, in this country
even in this antiseptic calmness.

In these well-ordered gardens,
sometimes a glimpse of a tail
of the King slithering, an angry thunderstorm
music to your fierce dancing.

Sometimes the sun scorches,
sometimes floods ravage.
The Destroyer in you.

But it's comforting,
whether in anger or in calmness
to see Shiva in this land
to know the all-pervading
everything of Shiva here, as in that
distant Himalayan land.

The God of Happiness

Wars rage in countries, battlefields grow.
Wars rage in human hearts, killings happen
in words, deeds, bodies.

The Earth dances its own *tandava*.
Hidden in the skies, unheeding,
sits the God of Happiness,
blue bodied, golden robed.
He shines in rainbows.
He giggles in super moons.
He dazzles in the sun's rays.

He bestows benedictions
laughingly, indiscriminately
in our outstretched palms
when we ask.
Some receive quivering moments
some receive lifetimes' blessings
some bewildered by his gaze
forget prayers and nurse despair.

He gives
when we give up
and ask.

Tandava: The divine dance of Lord Shiva is the tandava. There are at least seven forms of the tandava, depending on the mood of Lord Shiva, for example, he dances the anand tandava when he is happy. However, the more usual description of tandava is the dance of destruction when Shiva is angry about something, for example grave injustice. When Shiva dances this form of 'rudra' tandava, the world shakes and may be destroyed.

Shrine

A shrine of my past
hangs on the wall
at the back of the room
in a secret alcove.

I pay homage every day
to the memory
to the shrine
treasure it, a secret to disclose
only to those close enough
to move beyond the threshold.
A secret shared, a symbol of friendship
a reward for closeness.

I stitch my sorrows
into the shrine,
not knowing a shrine grows
out of the alcove,
into the room,
outside the house,
permeating life
until memory becomes reality.

To cast it away like a deity
worship over, into a river
with flowers, fire and incense
to forget, to let go
and reduce its potency.

Now, the shrine lives, grows
its tendrils
breathes life into sorrow

eternal.

Wholeness

How do you make yourself whole again?
When the toes are bitten
shredded as it were.
When the elbows are grazed
the bone showing.
When the fingers are cut
stumps exposed, blood
flowing freely.

Medicines, fillers, transplants,
but can you become, whole again?
Bring back aspirations, ideals
to become whole, again?

Tribals dance in the moonlight
amidst the cries of tigers, wolves.
Loneliness, darkness, emptiness,
eternal companions, lovers, twins inseparable.
The mad jungle thrives.
Where is my soul?
Where is compassion, love?

Boundaries blur.
The mirror taunts me at times
slow taunts about what was, and what is now.
Whole is a concept merely
completeness is only in the *Om*.

In the lives of today,
it's the incompleteness, the madness
to be sieved through, to find the meaning.

Om: the divine word; the most important spiritual symbol and mantra in Hinduism

Prayer

I have with me
a beautiful shoe but a broken foot.

A smile but no mouth
where do I wear my happiness?

In a silent prayer to You
I try to fold my hands.

My arms are cut at the wrists
knobbly stumps of flesh remain.

I try to shut my eyes
but the eyelashes are torn
and the edges bleeding.

I have in my heart a prayer
but nothing to offer it with.

Destiny

Seeing others do
I too rushed to fill Life.
Families, jobs, marriages, babies,
gifts given to all.

Not knowing that
a one legged man walked on graves,
ghosts cackled in trees,
white geese turned red,
on the day I was born.

Mothering lifeless children,
hacking rocks to walk a few steps,
praying every minute to continue a breath.

Unknown to me,
this was my destiny.

Despair

What is the colour of despair?
The smell of despair?

Hospitals, phenyl clean,
tubes, plastic, infections, masks,
blood, slicing knives, chemotherapy
for healthy and cancerous cells.

Like the slow dripping of water,
droplets of fear, rivulets
cutting deep, slicing through.
The knowledge of destiny,
irrevocable, inescapable.

When evenings turn into long nights
and weekends bring another day
of emptiness, childlessness.

What is the colour of despair?
Thick brown and grey,
yellowing in eyes
as I apply coats of Lancome mascara.

Whispers

Losing my step,
the times I have dreamed
the times I have hoped
and begged – Please, please, please
Not sure about what,
not sure to whom
faceless Gods of beyond
known Gods in temples.
But please, please, help, help
just living, just smiling
and thinking.
Just one original thought
the one sentence which
will fire words into a passion
force me into living
just please, please, please.

Voices call out to me
come on, come here
to be soothed, to be caressed.
But I know there is nothing
there is no one there, no one.

Just my own voice implores
into the encompassing space
Please, please, please.

Atonement

Do I beg rebirth?
Atone with a thousand dips
in those holy rivers,
mounts of purity
chanted by pilgrims
fanatic in belief,
the ones I had mocked.
Take back all that I ever chastised
or was in contempt of?

Goddesses in bright yellow sarees,
dark faces, red-hot vermillion smeared,
golden flowers adorning notches in trees,
mini temples dotting roadsides to protect
the millions in the country.
Those wayside shrines
I had never bowed to.

Should I retrace my steps?
This time with burning incense
and coconuts bursting with juice
when cracked open, white on a stone,
revisiting the fragments of my past.
Where can I find forgiveness?

If sorrow is the result of past sins
I do not remember having committed,
how do I atone
in this inevitable path to death
carrying a body which was given to me
incomplete, defective?

Will atonement bring completeness?

Nowhere to Go

Who will take care of her?
The wild-eyed woman
with the untamed hair?

You can see her at times
if you just go closer
or have the heart to accept
the anger, the passion in
the wild-eyed woman
with long forking nails

I hide her as best as I can
with coiffured hair, weekly manicures.
Lay cutlery and light candles at dinner
draw lace curtains below heavy velvet
just like them, normal women
gentle and accepting.

But when I cross my legs,
I see the scales of her belly
rippling
in anger, annoyed
always annoyed
with the dead men at the window.

This wild-eyed woman
Where will she go?
Where can she go?

Woman

I am no different from you,
homeless, grey *saree* in tatters,
matted hair, uncombed, unoiled for weeks
bindi smeared, vapid eyes
running through streets
to the cries of a mad woman
crying for the son killed in a street fight
ten years ago.

I too have buried my flesh.

I am no different from you,
in glittering cocktail dresses
red *sarees*, shiny blouse,
see through petticoats,
crimson gleaming lipstick, flowers
clipped on scented black hair,
stoned in public
for the lack of morality.

I too have traded my flesh.

I am no different from you,
attacked when defenceless
touched when asking not to be
nails gouging eyes out
but always failing
to stronger biceps
blood, oozing slowly
a victim's vulnerability.

I too have plunderers on my flesh.

Always, a different name,
a different country,
a different life.
But the same I.

Sarees: Indian costume
Bindis: traditionally, in India, a red dot worn on the forehead as a sign of marriage. -Now also a fashion accessory.

The Punishment

To be a child,
and know that arms will hold
voices will comfort
when you are scared.
That a mother's love is yours to claim
that a father's pride is yours to own.

To run into school
little back straight, head held high
knowing a day of wonder waits,
that the teacher's trust is yours.

Then, to be that child
of only six, punished
uncomprehending of the crime
which had to be atoned for.
Locked in a room and found by
familiar faces not to offer freedom
but hurt and violate
with devil hands, perverse bodies.

Did she think this was some hide and seek
I find you game?
Did she think, this too was
the teacher's way of punishing her?

Then to return home
unknowing of the devastation
and see your mother bleed in sorrow
your father break in anger.

Some of us are human still.

We weep in anguish,
scream in defiance.

We wilt in grief, knowing
nothing, nothing can repair
the one chance of childhood.
That once broken
nothing can rebuild
the spire of the dreams of tomorrow
that rises in every child's eyes.

(Written for the six- year-old girl raped by a teacher in Bangalore, India; unfortunately not the first, not the last)

Next Poem is b*ased on the painting 'The Metamorphosis of Narcissus' by Salvador Dali*

Metamorphosis

Narcissus sits transfixed
head bowed, limbs folded
watching a water spirit, he thinks.
Watching and loving and calling
a form like no other.
Nymph or spirit who loved before,
they wait for him, invite him back.
Forms naked in desire, in bodies.
Echo weeps and calls out.
They ask him to return from the lake
yet transfixed he sits
and pines and loves what cannot love him back.

He waits and he sinks
into himself, gaunt and lonely
into the lake reflecting
mountains, the world, his love.
Until the skies break into colour.
Until the earth weeps red.
Until his head implodes.
Cracks appear,
his body moulds into stone.

The rock he sits on
forms a giant hand
holding a cracked egg.
A narcissus blooms
hesitantly white,
deepening yellow,
forever brightening spring.

Nympheas

The lilies brood
darkening thoughts of what is past,
of what may never come,
dread rising silently
in stagnant roots.

The lilies weave
pink, purple, blue, flickers of
dreams, of wishes, of holding
bits of the sky in their bodies.

The lilies wilt
drooping lives, death the sentinel
standing close.

The lilies bloom
magic on paper, colours in the water,
impressions forming, growing, breaking
the canvas ablaze with a day, a season
and just for a moment
the lilies hold
eternity in their bodies.

(Based on the waterlilies series by Claude Monet)

Opera Garnier

Gilt-edged opulence, red velvet thickness,
the epitome of luxury
walking up wide balustrades
craning to see the vastness
the height of the ceiling, the roundness of the walls.
A door leading into the auditorium
the centre stage, the *raison de etre*
grandeur that is the Palais Garnier.

Paris lives outside unmindful;
changing traffic lights
rebellious pedestrians who walk
when the lights are green, and fast cars
which move when their lights are red
impervious of the glory
the monument rooted in their midst.

The stage with modern lights
a group of workers inspect it,
before the performance tonight.

To be a performer here
bowed to by the elegance
in the audience!
To hold the attention
To be the ambience!

Or be one of the audience
artistic, beautiful.
To come with a lover
decorated in chic jewels
a red sheath dress, a stole on the shoulders
secure with the promise of a long night
filled with embraces and passion.

If not,
I am content to stand here
with the others,
stand among them
and quickly take pictures.
Digital camera forgotten in the hotel
I manage with an iphone.
Snippets of imensity
to be preserved as evidence
that I have seen more than four walls.

Aquarelle Flash

A pot of paint spills
inking the pale blue
a rich pink, a muted orange.

Golden strands backlight
the palette
as rainbow colours
come together
in a sensuous embrace.

A quadrille of colours
lifts the sky
mint freshness
infusing the cool air.

Dawn breaks.

Inside, they continue to sleep
Oblivious,
the smell of yesterday
clinging to damp eyelids,
beer filled snores
reverberating inside walls.

As Infinity smiles outside
for just a second.

The Passage of Time

Calais rolls before my eyes
speeding, green-grassed England
merging with France.
The Eurostar fleeting across countries
contiguous, similar,
smokeless, noiseless,
only a mild vibration
of being on a train.
A loud whisper growing
through these trees ready to shed colour
stripped bare for the winter.

The Docklands Light Railway
weaves through offices, skyscrapers,
stacked up flats, routine lives,
mealtimes, lovemaking, births, death,
unmanned at the helm.
Efficient, eternal transits,
only a lurch at times
of being on a train.

The metropolis sleeps, grows, expands
living, glorious, passionate city.

But the trains of yesteryears –
the Konarak Express trundling
from Bhubaneswar to Mumbai
changing languages, changing landscapes
black dust engraved on palms.

The trains of yesterday
Carried wonder from small towns
future-less to large cities
frontiers of a future dreamt.

They carried a child from platforms
housing the poor, sick, infirm,
the wealthy, proud, genuine.

On the way, horizons exploded,
sunrises gleamed, rains washed,
brushed clean, leaving promises,
dreams intact, to be consummated
years later,
in the silent trains of the future.

Konarak Express

Super-fast Konarak express
from Bhubaneswar to Bombay
thirty-five stops
thirty-seven hours and fifteen minutes
from East to West.

The choosing of the berths, the top
best to sleep longer, the middle, feeling unreal
existing at night, not at day
the lowest for those who couldn't, wouldn't
climb the narrow rungs to the top.

The claiming of the window seats
to look at pale blue skies
stretches of houses, sleepy towns
awakening as you did, when morning
arrived with its cries of tea
your mother already changed into a fresh *saree*
the smell of metal on your hands as you
held on to the window rails, looking out.
Looking out.

The big stop everyone knew, Vijaywada,
when you saw your father run out
to fill water, get tea in earthen cups,
samosas served in bowls of leaves.

Your eyes followed him
and you worried, and worried
the train would suddenly leave
without his form.

Thirty Kilometres

You lived in a rambling country house.
Thirty kilometres from the sea,
thirty kilometres from your school,
thirty kilometres from the town.
You grew up having buttery croissants
and hot chocolate for breakfast
and were driven to school
by your mum in a powder-blue car.

I grew up in the dusty plains.
Power cuts, *khus-khus* screens
to ward away the heat.
Travelled in rickshaws to school
with five other children
distance a nebulous concept
in my small town.

The seaside possibly
was about thirty kilometres
I told you once, in a desire
to find a common thread
in our pasts.

Some day if our bodies met
would they know
the distances, the differences?
Or would they come together
pasts, cultures, backgrounds melting
forming brave new futures?

Stranger Love

I know I must not feel
anything is different
after that day.
Though my hands, now
tendrils, wet and thick
grasping, stroking.
Though my legs, now
mermaid tails
glistening sea-green.
Though my lips
ripeness,
cavernous, bottomless.
Still, I mustn't remember
you were here
taking my weight
counting the spots on my back.
One, two, three, this is beautiful.

I mustn't notice as well
that outside the weeping willow is
sloping closer to the river.
That lotuses have sprung to the surface
of the pond, bright pink, lush.

Instead, I must forget
you were here at this window
that legs entwined around your waist
hands unrestrained, explored.
You don't like words you say
no use for something without form.

I must remember to not want more
for this was one time
fleeting so quickly
before a memory could be conceived.
I must know in my heart
That our worlds – I know no one in yours
you know no one in mine –
our worlds never for a moment met
and swooned into each other.
Nothing really happened.

A Call

Is that your voice?
The one which calls out
when the night and morning meet
and form the molten love-child, dawn.

Is that your voice?
Sometimes bird, sometimes human
at times a whisper, at times a shout.

It can only come from worlds across
over the hay- filled fields
the placid sheep
from caves, caverns or mountains
or beyond.

It questions, do you remember me?
It soothes, I will always be here.

Sometimes, it stands outside forgotten.

The Glass Jar

Embarrassed, I answer
when asked what I write about
love, longing, despair, sorrow.
Shamefacedly I say, it's poetry
of feelings, of touch,
of words, of moonlight,
creeping up the walls,
entering my mind.

But you are askance.
'Why do you want to, why write poetry?'
You throw open the windows
spanning your million pound flat
'Look at this, riches and more!
It's ours for the taking,
for loving.
There is so much to do!'

Our world is shiny
high boots, higher buildings.

Glittering cities, rotting souls, I think.

'Wasting your time means nothing.
Don't you see? Nothing!
Do, achieve!
This, and this and more.'

Dead words writhing on a page, I think.

'We should be in bed,' you continue.

My shoes are Louboutin red, beautiful
my clothes are Prada, fitting
now abandoned on the floor
near the shiny cream sofas.

I lie in bed
in perfumed sheets, feather duvets.
Words swim somewhere
in my heart, in my mind
like butterflies
trying in vain to escape.

Of the Night

The night is here
like floods on riverbanks
like creeping snow storms.
The night is here irrevocably
and in this night
You and I are cocooned.
The fabric holding us
skeins of hope and despair
interwoven.

We see it in ourselves
in our eyes, in our limbs
as we alternate between furious
and gentle embraces.
Lost souls find each other
but in this vastness
our fragile togetherness
like a Diwali *diya*
wavering, not knowing
when it will blow out
in the slightest breeze.

We make promises
sometimes we mean it.
Creatures writhing
lust or longing
or a deep desire to be one.
The night shrouds us
we try to stitch ourselves together.

Our shapeless frames
wilt as they enter the brightness
fall apart when the day beckons.

Diwali: Indian festival of lights
Diya: earthen candle lit with oil

A Fair Exchange

Your fingers stroke my hair
your smile is not brutal
as your lips bite into my neck
sharp and clean
drawing blood, vampire- like.

I know it must be done.

Love is in the caves
lost, lonely.
To find it and make it whole,
to clothe and wash it,
to adopt it –
It's not for everyone.

Only the brave receive manna,
only the ones who walk through fire
are redeemed.

Puny thoughts, shallow desires.
What can that bestow?

A slow drawing of blood
is not that bad.

In return,
a mansion, soft pile rugs on marble floors,
fox and rabbit fur nestling on my neck
glorious jewels shining, hiding the sharp bite.

I know when night comes
I will be back
in bed, with those fangs
telling myself, this is it.
This is love.

Blighted Knight

You are beautiful
no excess, hair, fat,
on your frame.
Slim as if to fit
through doorways, on couches
or other bodies.
Your fingers, long and perfect
unlike mine, big, with flat nails.

On your face, dimples bloom
as you smile.
On your cheeks, on your chin
the deep cleft disappears
and forms two smaller dimples.
When I touch them, I know
the shapes, changing
with your moods.
When you love
there are no excesses.
Sensations grow, no weight, no heaviness.

There must have been warning signs
somewhere, sometime.
A ripple in the pool
of darkness in you.
So cleanly you cut
away people.
Did it take years of practice?
No apology, no feelings
when words are lies.

What are you then
coward, callous, cruel?
Lover, blighted man
of the dimples and dark soul
why do I miss you still?

Happiness in Love

If we were Gods
we would have created,
golden red darting birds
blue grasshoppers
flowers which laugh
when tickled
music in mango trees.
We would in our happiness
draw a million rainbows over the earth.

If we were yogis
we would have meditated,
devotees would flock to us
marvel at our serenity
thank us for small miracles
and keep us next to the Gods.
We would in our happiness
walk with them, show them the way.

But as it is,
You are you, I am I
a mere man, a mere woman,
we hurt, we pleasure
we try everything
to be closer together
to keep the oneness
as long as we can
with candles, aroma, *tantra*.

Sometimes I think,
in our happiness
we are almost there.

*Tantra : ancient Indian tradition of beliefs and meditation
and ritual practices*

His Poem

He calls me '*Happiness*'
as if achievable, measurable
as if in my smiles, the world
rotates ceaselessly on its axis.
As if you can gather moonlight, sunlight
in your arms and stun them into a bouquet

What does he see?

Clouds form and shape
unicorns, dragons, lovers on the skies.
Fireflies light up limbs.
We look at them, we look at each other
and he calls me '*Happiness.*'
Not understanding I ask why?

What does he see?

As if a look can bloom rows
of roses, scented hyacinths, blow
sticky pollen from *kadamba* flowers.
As if arms can silence screams of the past
as if my touch is enough for him
to perfume his life, dust him with magic.

What does he see?

He calls me ' *Happiness'*
sinking feet, fettered arms
imperfect mouth, burning eyes, enraptured I
feel moments like beads on a necklace.
Fly, swim, love, live
hoping he always will.

Kadamba : a yellow, fragrant flower from India

His Gift

He doesn't need any gift, he says
just some lines, for him
specially written.

The lines I want to write, I want them
to shake the world
to trace the first rape, the first injustice
erase them forever.
To go back to the moment
they tore the world
and chastise them
move them to never doing so.

Write about love, he says.
Love is passé, who writes about love?
Didn't we decide to bury it
and forget where ?
Didn't we decide to abandon it
on the roadside, orphaned?
Didn't we then burn what was left
chanting to let the pyre rage?

My pen stops
when it starts to ink the past,
traces hearts, bodies lose boundaries
mere shapes.
We look out of the window
the deepening skies, the lightening moon
the lines solid.
We are content, we are hungry,
words soothe when nothing else can.

I want to write, if you pluck a lotus
feel the stalk, you will feel spiny, slimy
the pink richness of the petals.
If you open your eyes wide
pluck stars out, they will
float into a jar.
If you trace that mole on my shoulder,
the back will arch, fingers will touch limbs.

So close to the soul,
so close, only you.

Love Lost

Leaning over to me
he said
I know you, I know your smell
from times ago
of autumn leaves, of woods
of greenery, fireplaces.
Perhaps he was right

I asked
Is knowing loving?

Sitting next to me
he said
I have seen that smile
remember that voice
from my dreams of long ago
from childhood, from fantasy.
Perhaps he did

I asked
Is memory worth it?

Holding on to me
he said
I wouldn't change this
wouldn't change anything
just life, just this love.

I asked
Can love really be all?

I still ask the questions now
long after he has left
not knowing if the answer
has come and gone
or will ever return, again.

Ill-Fated Love

Do you remember
the train in India, the motion
the faint rumbling, soothing
as we slept all night?
I was on the middle berth
you on the lower
your fingers slipped through
the chink between the seat and walls
tapping, until I slipped my hand across.
Your hand closed on mine.

The train moved across hours, states
fingers interlinked we dreamt up futures
the usual, love, children, success
everything
the world has done before
countlessly, incessantly
feeling we are the first
to have thought of it.

Outside, clouds gathered
bats hanging low on trees
grew vampire teeth
ghosts rose in coffins and fires
to suck all the dreams
all the softness of that night.

Nostalgia

Where did you go rainbow-winged
bird of flight?

Seen lost in slumber
or when sleep filled eyes awaken
transient rays of the early sun.
Enraptured with memories,
Krishna- blue, *Lakshm*i-gold
dazzling eyes.

Just a flash of those wings,
just a whiff of an earthy smell
enough to coat days with dreams.

I used to see you nest
beyond those mango trees
where rainforests grow lush beyond realms
where longing mates with dreams.

I look out of the window, waiting.
On the window sill, a Murano vase stands
green yellow purple, colour medley
frozen in its middle
cold, unmoving.

I arrange soft flowers
still looking out of the window,
looking out of my life
as the horizon
drifts further away,
as a flash of colour
fades into greyness.

Krishna: Beautiful Hindu God, an avatar of Vishnu, with blue-black skin. Vishnu being part of the Holy Trinity, the preserver
Lakshmi: Beautiful Hindu Goddess of wealth

Jealousy

She of the tiara, of stars in her hair,
of moonlight, silken gowns,
of the sun transforming her house into shining
heavens,
she of the beauty, which lustrously invaded her
husband's mind
and other parts restlessly every night; she the owner of
artefacts, jewellery, from shops, online
brought in by ships from exotic countries
with unpronounceable names.

She of the beauty and riches,
saw others with dimples laughing in their cheeks
brighter stars than hers in their eyes, slimmer waists,
softer breasts,
songs in their steps, taller houses and wider gardens,
and she made sure they were not around her anymore.

She saw her child laugh louder in the company of
others
even more than in hers, so she snatched the smile away
to hide in a little red box studded with shiny mirrors.

She prodded and carved out the eyes of one, the heart
of another,
the friendship of the generous, she marvelled at her
claws
growing faster and sharper by the day
to gouge out what should have been hers.
She hid them in coloured boxes and kept them in
drawers
safely, to look upon as hers every day.

Much later, she saw her skin had turned *salak* like,
snakes mated in her hair.
When she laughed, blood dribbled from the sides.
The boxes when opened were empty
dried kernels of nothingness –
and she wondered why.

Salak: snake fruit; fruit found mostly in Indonesia with scaly skin.

Midlife Crisis

Grow your own vegetables,
plant climbing roses, clematis,
write, complete a creative course,
travel around the world,
exercise, exercise, exercise,
eat salads only,
try for the first time, some cannabis
learn to salsa
Learn to live?
win the lottery
have a baby.
Muddled, confused, thoughts
milling together
modern day fighting with the old
Gaugin, Monet
prisms, trapeziums
the things never tried
a threesome
Yoga?
Meditation,
restlessness, hoping, killing,
buy another house
in millions this time, trademark
en-suite bathrooms, tiled granite
drive, and confidently.

When the questions are not asked
the answers do not form.
When everything seems inadequate
and futility grows, was this it?
Was this enough? Did I do myself proud?
Did I make anyone proud?
Or could it all have been different?

Perfection

Give me some time
I will write it yet.
After I paint the walls of my study
a mellow cream
place soft cuddly cushions
with rose covers on the floor
frame my picture of Monet's lilies
for the walls.
I will write it yet –
The perfect poem

I will be there yet
almost there.
Give me some time
yes, just move a little bit to the side
hold me there, that's about right
Where is your passion?
I am almost there

It could have been perfect,
is that television on again?
The mundane blocks perfection.

Childlessness

I have travelled across seas
walked in deserts
flown over mountains
fallen from skies
lived in the arms
of strong men
watched the hunt of
helpless large kudus
felt the love of raging elephants.

I have done it all.

When can I have you
to hold, to watch
as you sleep
to love you as no other?

Travelled worlds
owned diamonds
possessed and loved.

When do I get lucky
like my harassed neighbour
Mother of four?

My Children

The boy who went away
would have been today
aged six.
The girl who never came
would have been today
aged two.

The story of my children.
Children of the past and the future
never seen in the present.
Their souls entwined with mine
as part of their destiny and mine
to not live in this world.

Nothing is enough
to change
the minds of souls.
Souls which decide when to come
when to leave.
Bibs, beanies, baby smells
remain behind in empty arms.

The boy who went away.
The girl who never came.
There is lamentation
there are tears of sorrow.
Finally forced acceptance in the
cliché of all times
that time heals all
or at least coats bleeding wounds
with thick scabs.

Advice to My Unborn Daughter

My dear little one, my dear Miliani,
born brown as warm earth,
head filled with hair black as kohl
these Indian signs I cannot change
but the small things I can.

As I tuck you in every night,
will place a pink flower on your pillow,
draw a star on your feet,
braid your hair with beads and glitter.
Will paint a picture
of you on a white horse
riding in Hyde Park
on a Sunday morning
the air washed clean
from rains before.
Hair streaming behind you,
straight-backed and proud,
queen of what you see.

And when they come for you
as surely they will, with red bangles,
vermilion pots for your hair
and ask to drape yourself in sarees
sacrifice and live in devotion,
receive in return
a lifetime of love and respect,
promise me my child
you will not forget
me, the vision, our vision
of flight, rain, wind,
whipping through trees
sorcerer like.

You will swim as always
graceful as a ballet dancer
and teach your daughter to do the same.

*Vermillion: red powder worn in the hair-parting by a
married woman*

Motherhood

My beautiful baby boy asleep
with dreams, smiles,
little sighs, sometimes a whimper
as if he's run into a doorway
seen something he doesn't like.
My little baby boy fast asleep
and looking at him I wonder:

Did I do anything good to deserve him?
Do I do anything good to deserve him?

My wonderful baby boy
running, chasing a ball
orange, blue
an adept kick and a
surprised look from passers-by.
Looking at him run I hope:

Let me have done something good to deserve him
Let me be doing something good to deserve him.

My heroic baby boy
miraculously born, perfect and whole.
Seeing his smile wondrous I pray:

Let me deserve him
Let me always deserve him.

Carousel

The blue dinosaur sits duck-like
on its fat tummy, squat
looks into the eyes of the smaller animals
a green spotty turtle, a baby hippopotamus
an orange elephant and a yellow giraffe
hanging down on a mobile
moving carousel-like to
'It's a wonderful world'
The favourites in my baby's world.

Shadows on the ceiling
hold special promise
shiny knobs, brass door handles
wonderful pieces to examine
soft monkeys, noisy ducks.
In a baby's world
everything is amazing.

We worry about jobs, pension funds,
bills to pay, people to call
and when the baby looks up

mouth open in an O
we rearrange drooping mouths
and wear brilliant-smile facades.

Reassured, baby plays on.

In Search of Balance

Yet another hotel room
impersonal, indistinct
sameness.

I check the soaps and the lotions
and add them to my growing collection.

I fluff out the beds to make it more slept in
and try to make the night shorter by staying out late.

Anything to make it quick,
anything to forget
the little crying face I left behind.

The joy of achievement,
the sorrow of seeing a child cry.

As stillness grows in the hotel room,
I wish you a good night's sleep miles away
and lie awake until dawn drops.

Kiss of Tragedy

When tragedy comes
and kisses you on the mouth
the ones outside are the most upset.
For us, hugged close by tragedy
there are the same chores
the same shops with discounts
on the larger packets of biscuits
The routines for dinner, lunch and the rest.

Others stare with disgust
'Arms hang from their sockets shredded ligaments
You wipe off the blood and carry on as before.
How could you come to this?
For surely this would never happen to me.'

But only this moment matters
The present exists; past tragedy or a living tragedy
you are used to the beating heart of the monster
It lives with you, intimately.

When they tell you the perfunctory
'You are brave, you are doing well.'
You are askance, surely this existence
of intensity, of raw pain is life.

Institutionalised, you live within realms.

Words

At best, I hope to string you along
in a kind of sequence
a canto, a sonnet, or an ode.
Give you a name
try to make you rhyme.
>But you lie there, broken
>coarsening bits of memory
>feelings quivering in the sun
>then wilting and dying
>like so much more does.

Can there be anything else
beyond the Wasteland?
Can there be any more poetry
in this burial chamber of words
and should it be written?
>I dream, I think, I walk
>I luxuriate, I sleep
>I beg, I implore
>I shrivel, I die
>I die, wanting more from you.

Rest! Sit at peace!
Form yourself into garlands
into wondrous bouquets of tiger lilies tied
with white satin ribbons
whip yourselves into
a soft cherry red cake.
>But you sit there
>just outside the boundary
>of where my brain meets ether
>reality meets nothingness
>maddeningly alone, stubbornly aloof
>you sit there taunting me to desperation.

Wilful, disobedient words
which are mine, but never mine to form as I wish
control as I wish.
Colour into tapestries, stitch into patchwork quilts
cook into velvety soups
of lentils, meat, vegetables, mixing bone with mush.
Words strewn like stones, out of my grasp
independent of each other.
        And as my mind paints the vastness
        up to the skies in vivid red, orange
        my words remain unconceived
        or are born stunted, deformed progeny
        of my imagination and passion.

We Write in Vain

Words appear on paper
at ease, as if they haven't been deliberated,
thought of, reasoned.
As if they haven't been found deep
within the memories of blood
the pain of the bones
the shadow of skin.
As if they haven't been
drawn from the past,
the one imagined
the one spent.
Words live on paper,
as if it has been easy
to find them
as if forwarded on whastapp
as if they haven't been chased
to the moon on horseback
on glittery mountain roads
or slipped through fingers
silvery fish in a net,
pined, lusted, worked for.

Words live verdant
on the tongue
ready to walk away.
On the edges of the fingers
waiting to coil and jump
on immortal paper.

Know this:
none of the above needs to happen.
A poem – for what is it
but words fancifully
decorating paper?
A story – what is it
but imagined lies?

Know this:
poetry, stories
are just easy craft
of the fanciful.

Dreams

They hang from the trees,
they grow from the earth
pushing through gently.
If you find them, oh,
if you find them,
you must seize them
hide them behind your eyes.
You must softly, softly seed them
in your heart,
they live long orchid-like.
They may even flower
dazzling you in surprise.

If the days are spent,
and you haven't seen them
 flashing through the skies
laughing in oceans,
and you don't know yet
a dream from a non-dream,
then look inside.
Within the crevices of brains,
within the glistening blood,
scrape under the skin,
tear out the nails
and strip the roots of your hair.

And somewhere, surely somewhere,
you will find it.
Shrivelled perhaps, distorted perhaps,
tiny, so tiny as to be missed,
but shining with its potency.
A dream.

Ruins

I see a building
stroked by neglect, kissed by moss
for years.
I see families
bags of the past abandoned
departing for shores further.
I see iron ripping
through the concrete, the walls
criss-crossing cracks.

Ruin
Inevitable ruin.
When the future arrives
the past has to leave.
It is the way.

They still see
silks on the floors, swords on the walls,
the glory of the past glistening
still
in the overgrown garden,
the broken down kitchen.
They talk of
shining spheres hanging from the rafters
where pigeons roost now
golden orbs bought from
foreign lands.

We leave,
pride in their eyes
holding on, holding on to
what is no more.
We leave,
pictures of ruins in my lenses
crumbling, fading sepia.

What is Lost

Children, often little girls, go missing
voiceless in a labyrinth.
Planes go missing
in unchartered trajectories.
Memories go missing
in vacant souls.

The words nestling in my heart
released in my breath go
missing.
I hold up my hands
in the air, to find the very air is
missing.

In Memory

They told me the pen is mightier than the sword
I know for sure, they did.
Maybe in second grade, or the third.
The teacher asked – What do you understand by this phrase?
Please explain in ten lines, as part of classwork
as part of homework.
We always knew, we always believed
the pen, rising above the blood, the horror,
the pen, nimble and true, the pen always stronger.

For his pen, he died, for his drawings, he bled.
For their belief, they perished.
For their spirit, they fell.

And so did we.
In our homes, in our planes, in our cars, in our shops,
we burned, we suffered, we walked, we vigilled,
we too hurt in small ways.

The pen is mightier than the sword.
It is.
I know, for they've told me so.
Never mind if today it is broken,
never mind if ink has turned blood,
never mind if we cry for families bereft,
never mind if we mourn talent lost,
lives extinguished, fear birthed.
Never mind, never mind, never mind.

We will win, we have to win
for the pen lives supreme, the pen draws,
the pen grows, the pen vanquishes.
Swords, bullets, blind obsessions, maniac actions.
For I was told, for I always believe,
the mighty pen, the pen glorious.

Je suis Charlie.

Shiver up a Spine

He was given names at birth
baby, sugar, honey, sweetie-pie,
names that could curdle milk
sweeter than cupcakes
or *rasogollas* and *laddoos*.
(depending on preferences)
Cloistered in furs and woolly hats
he was fed rice with a silver spoon
he was everything, the esteemed
waited on hand and feet, he had to be perfect
in every way, to become.

He was simply a shiver waiting for a spine to run up.

School, college years, he learnt to be noble
to speak the correct tense, perfect grammar
inflection, the correct accent
(depending on where you have lived)
in modelled clothes and appearance
he was trying hard.

He was simply a shiver waiting for a spine to run up.

When the time came, when the world asked him
for an opinion, for money, for anything
as it always does
when the soldiers were sent away
the doctors were busy treating
when the teachers were told to teach the unspeakable
when he was asked to stand for what is to be done
or not done
(depending on what you do)
he was askance, not knowing, not caring
dulled thoughts, rusty actions.

For he was simply a shiver waiting for a spine to run up.

(Based on the quote by Paul Keating)
Rasogollas, laddoos: Indian sweets

People, Unlike Fish

Do not die like that, just like that.

Found floating on top of the pond
rigid, fins moving in the breeze
without warning.

A single fish
floats rigid while the rest
circle, waiting for their food
oblivious of the dead
stiff, eyes transfixed
as if in horror.

People unlike fish
don't need to be
hastily disposed of, burnt
 or buried
under the soft earth.

When people die, surely
there will be a tweet, #departed.
Their Skype will close
their Facebook status updated to dead
their voicemail will proclaim
I am not available in the world.

The earth will shriek
the trees will weep
craters will form and fill with blood.
You will hear it in your soul first
when someone you know dies.

Yes, people unlike fish
do not die like that, suddenly
without warning.

The Visit

I know your touch by now
when you enter so quietly
so completely, the footsteps soft.
I know how you fan your fingers
on a loved one's face and take away
their thoughts their breath their love
their fingers their toes their all that is to us.

I know the days after, sudden grief
the calls from relatives, friends,
the commiserations, the questions.
I know how suddenly a pit carves itself
slicing into our lives
how we throw rituals funerals flowers
thoughts prayers; bottomless pit
we paint what we can't fill.

We think of the rainbow
we spotted as you left,
the tears of a doctor who failed,
the love of a stranger who held our hand.

We smile when raindrops shower
as we immerse fragments of our loved one
in an urn in the seas.

We remember Hindu philosophy,
death, souls reborn.
We wait for another life
thinking this is it. Beautiful death,
lovely, romantic, philosophical
making love to our thoughts.

But I know You – Death.

How after weeks months years
the calm disappears
the fingerprints you branded on our hearts
sears at night; in its corners, in the darkness,
wet earth suffocates,
winds storm, skeletal faces gape
in your wake.

The pincers you leave crush the heart.
There is only starkness,
gaunt hollowed faces.
The shadows are bloodied,
the skies remain angry.

How the mind craves, the heart desires.
How we miss them forever!
How you never let us forget your visit
Death.

Immersion

(For my father, 9th July 2009)

These steps, unimagined, unthinkable,
at this time, too soon, not expected.
These rocks, black, ragged, slippery,
from the beating sea waves.
I deftly jump rock to rock, sure-footed, unafraid
holding this urn, precious,
covered in a checked red and white cloth
care-wrapped .
Those behind thinking perhaps she will slip
perhaps she won't be able to throw it out wide.

I have carried the urn from its place in the little puja room
close to my heart; to the ashram, on my lap
holding on to make up that I never saw you when you went away
when you shut your eyes and fell down, when you decided to leave
I was miles away, all of five-thousand at my computer, on a phone.
An unusual storm, almost tropical, with its tumultuous rain
silvery lightning and cascading thunder
raged through an otherwise calm England.
When they took you away from home, when they laid you on a fire
I wasn't there, but this pot is real, and is mine.
Today it is my childhood, the stories you'd told
the toy-cars, the doll-houses you made, the uniforms you ironed
the immaculate packages addressed in your neat writing.
The nights you stayed awake that I could sleep
unhindered by your snoring.
Memories snuggle against each other.

We unwrap the cloth now, empty the urn
and I see some bones, a part of you;

one slightly coloured as if with fresh blood.
The same bones, the blood in me, it lives on.
Then we place flowers on you
roses, marigold, red, gold, beautiful; light incense sticks
smoke swirls over jagged rocks.
I touch your bones, broken bits of bones, precious
wait for a sign, to tell me you are here, nearby.

My toddler sleeps peacefully in his bed
knowing his grandfather is now a star.
I feel no older than him, I feel as old as I can ever become
I see your gait in his run.

It is a beautiful day, here on the seaside.
I could run on miles of these rocks, barefoot.
I could wake up hours earlier.
I could live forever on these bland meals,
I have been having for the past ten days
learn to love the harsh sun, the dust,
the crowds I ran away from.

I want to do this for you, I worry if I did enough
did I do enough, did I let you down? Ever?

I must let go, they say. Throw my red cloth away
into the ocean with the next wave. Now.
I do, with all my force, balancing on the rocks
but you decide to come back.
They come forward to help throw my bond away
This time you decide to float, away and near, back and
forth
on those waves. We watch for a while.

Your blue fleece waits in England, in the cupboard at home
The one you wore all day
until I said, we must get a new one.

We watch you float, you seem to be enjoying it
I will stay here, until you decide to leave.
But gently I am drawn away by a hand on my shoulder.
I look back:
friends, cousins, uncles, aunts
a beautiful mother, here, united in shock.

The fishing boats are out, the sea is gentle
the sun still not its harsh self in Pondicherry
and there on the blueness, the red cloth nestling
one today with this vastness.

A perfect immersion.
You are gone, but you are home.

Other books by Skylark Publications UK

Word Masala 2011 ISBN 9780956084019
An anthology of poems and short stories by the South-Asian diaspora writers and poets

Bottled Ganges ISBN 9780956084002
A collection of poems by Yogesh Patel

Word Masala Award Winners 2016 ISBN 9780956084033
An anthology featuring poems by Word Masala Award winners

Some of the 100 past issues of Skylark magazine were special numbers. They are available to collectors or researchers at £75 each by a special order. Please request a list.

Non-fictions

Free Accounting with Free Software ISBN 9780956084026
This book by Yogesh Patel prepares you for book-keeping and accounting with the recommended, tested and compliant free software.

All available from our website at
www.skylarkpublications.co.uk

Or
www.consultants4vat.co.uk

Word Masala Foundation

The foundation promotes South-Asian diaspora poets and writers by awarding them for their excellence in poetry.

Instead of a monetary prize, it helps by working as a non-commercial agent for them, helping with the reviews, highlighting their work through its publications and magazines, organising readings and programmes, and placing articles and interviews where possible.

The foundation is a non-commercial thrust and believes very strongly in working with our Western counterparts. It recognises all good work they do as struggling small and large presses. For that, it awards them with a recognition plaque highlighting their efforts in diversity. We work to help them for the books by South-Asian diaspora poets and writers.

You can also help by joining our growing list of subscribers and by buying books by our award-winning poets and writers.

Director
Yogesh Patel

Consultant Editor
Dr Debjani Chatterjee MBE

Patrons
Lord Parekh
Lord Dholakia